BY MYSELF

For Patsy —

For quiet times!

BY MYSELF

Poems selected by LEE BENNETT HOPKINS
Illustrations by GLO COALSON

Thomas Y. Crowell
New York

For Pat Allen

BY MYSELF

Text copyright © 1980 by Lee Bennett Hopkins
Illustrations copyright © 1980 by Glo Coalson
For information address Crowell Junior Books, 10 East 53rd Street,
New York, N.Y. 10022. Published simultaneously in Canada by
Fitzhenry & Whiteside Limited, Toronto.

Designed by Ellen Weiss

Library of Congress Cataloging in Publication Data
Main entry under title:

By myself.

  SUMMARY: A selection of poems reflecting a child's
view of school, family relations, nature, being alone,
and self.
  1. Children's poetry, American. [1. American
poetry—Collections] I. Hopkins, Lee Bennett. II.
Coalson, Glo.
PS586.B96   811'.008   79-7830
ISBN 0-690-04070-9
ISBN 0-690-04071-7 (lib. bdg.)

1   2   3   4   5   6   7   8   9   10
First Edition

Acknowledgments

Addison-Wesley Publishing Company, Inc., for "Up in the Pine." Reprinted from *Blueberries Lavendar*, copyright © 1977 by Nancy Dingman Watson, by permission of Addison-Wesley Publishing Company, Inc.

Atheneum Publishers, Inc., for "Pretending to Sleep" from *Flashlight and Other Poems* by Judith Thurman, copyright © 1976 by Judith Thurman, and "Until I Saw the Sea" from *I Feel the Same Way* by Lilian Moore, copyright © 1967 by Lilian Moore. Used by permission of Atheneum Publishers.

Joanna Cole for "Driving to the Beach." Used by permission of the author who controls all rights.

Thomas Y. Crowell, Publishers, for "So Will I" from *River Winding: Poems by Charlotte Zolotow*. Text copyright © 1970 by Charlotte Zolotow. By permission of Thomas Y. Crowell, Publishers.

Curtis Brown, Ltd., for "In the Pitch of the Night" by Lee Bennett Hopkins, copyright © 1979 by Lee Bennett Hopkins, and "Boy on the Bus" by Lee Bennett Hopkins, copyright © 1979, 1980 by Lee Bennett Hopkins.

Elsevier-Dutton Publishing Company, Inc., for "Wings" from *Me Is How I Feel* by Stacy Jo Crossen and Natalie Ann Covell. Copyright © 1970 by A. Harris Stone, Stacy Crossen, Natalie Covell, Victoria deLarrea. By permission of the publisher, E. P. Dutton.

Harper & Row, Publishers, Inc., for an excerpt from *Near the Window Tree: Poems and Notes by Karla Kuskin*. Copyright © 1975 by Karla Kuskin. By permission of Harper & Row, Publishers, Inc.

Florence Parry Heide for "Rocks." Used by permission of the author who controls all rights.

Instructor Publications, Inc., for "Think of It" by Bette Killion. Reprinted from *Instructor*, copyright © February 1978 by the Instructor Publications, Inc. Used by permission.

Little, Brown and Company for "The Star in the Pail," copyright © 1952 by David McCord, and "Gone," copyright © 1970 by David McCord. Reprinted from *One at a Time* by David McCord, by permission of Little, Brown and Company.

McIntosh and Otis, Inc., for "Tomorrow" from *A Crazy Flight and Other Poems* by Myra Cohn Livingston. Copyright © 1969 by Myra Cohn Livingston. Reprinted by permission of McIntosh and Otis, Inc.

Charles Scribner's Sons for "The Child Who Cried" and "When I Am Me" from *I Hear You Smiling and Other Poems* by Felice Holman. Copyright © 1973 by Felice Holman. Used by permission of Charles Scribner's Sons.

CONTENTS

WINGS

Down away
Out away
Fly out of school.

It's dark here
It's dull here
It's sunny outside.
Today's long
The work's hard
I don't like to spell.
My head hurts
My hand aches
The wind's rushing by—

So, down away
Out away
Fly out of school.

The clock says
It's two hours
Before we can leave.
I just want
To run wild
And play for an hour.
Not sit here
This afternoon
Dreaming along—

Down away
Out away
Fly out of school.

I'll make...
Slides to slide
Ropes to climb
Wings to fly free.
I'll plan...
Ways to go
Things to do
Friends I can see.
I'll find...
Jokes to tell
Laughs to laugh
Kings I can be—

Oh, down away
Out away
Fly out of school.

　　But
I laugh here
I joke here
I play with my friends.
I think here
I listen and
Hear stories of kings.
It's good to be
Here sometimes.
Then I don't want to be—

Down away
Out away
Far out of school.

—Stacy Jo Crossen and Natalie Anne Covell

BOY ON THE BUS

was reading
Snow White and the Seven Dwarfs

when a man in a seat nearby
said,

"Snow White?
Snow White is a girl's book."

And the boy
replied
without looking up from the page,

"But the dwarfs are all men!"

And
he
continued
reading.

—*Lee Bennett Hopkins*

THINK OF IT

"Go quickly," says my mother
or some other
hurry person.
   Then I think of fast things—
      hummingbird wings
      lizards darting
      racers starting
      bicycle wheels
      automobiles
      wind through the trees
      some angry bees—
  and I'm quick!

"Sh-h-h!" says my mother
or some other
tiptoe person.
   Then I think of still things—
      empty swings
      dark nights
      soaring kites
      thick, soft mittens
      newborn kittens
      whispered prayers
      sleeping bears—
  and I'm quiet!

"Slow down," says my mother
or some other
getting tired person.
 Then I think of lazy things—
  yawning kings
  elephants strolling
  plump pigs rolling
  a cow chewing cud
  some oozing mud
  inchworm on my hand
  sifting sand—
and I go slow!

—Bette Killion

from
NEAR THE WINDOW TREE

Where
Have you been dear?
What
Have you seen dear?
What
Did you do there?
Who
Went with you there?
Tell me
What's new dear?
What's
New with you dear?
Where
Will you go next?
What
Will you do?

"I do this and I do that.
I go here and I go there.
At times I like to be alone.
There are some thoughts that are my own
I do not wish to share."

—Karla Kuskin

THE CHILD WHO CRIED

I found a cave
I found a cave
    deep
    deep
    deep
and went inside
and went inside
    to sleep
    sleep
    sleep
and dreamed a dream
and dreamed a dream
    deep
    deep
    deep
about a child who always cried
about a child who always cried
    weep
    weep
    weep
Then I awoke
    Then I awoke
        bright, bright, bright
    and climbed outside
    and looked about
    and saw the sky
    and shouted, "I
    am *not* the child who cried!"

—*Felice Holman*

UP IN THE PINE

I'm by myself
I want to be
I don't want anyone
Playing with me

I'm all alone
In the top of the pine
Daddy spanked me
And I don't feel fine

I can look way out
On the woods and lakes
I can hear the buzz
That the chain saw makes

And a woodpecker chopping
In the crabapple tree
With his red crest bobbing
But he doesn't see me

If anybody hollers
I'll pretend I'm not there
I may miss dinner
But I don't care

The pine needles swish
And the wind whistles free
And up in the pine
Is only me

It's starting to rain
But the tree keeps me dry
We toss in the black clouds
The tree and I

Now Daddy's calling.
He never *stays* mad.
He probably feels awful
Because I'm sad.

I'll answer Daddy.
He's concerned about the weather.
I'll climb down and he'll take my hand
And we'll go in the house together.

—*Nancy Dingman Watson*

DRIVING TO THE BEACH

On the road
smell fumes and tar
through the windows
of the car.

But at the beach
smell suntan lotion
and wind
    and sun
        and ocean!

—*Joanna Cole*

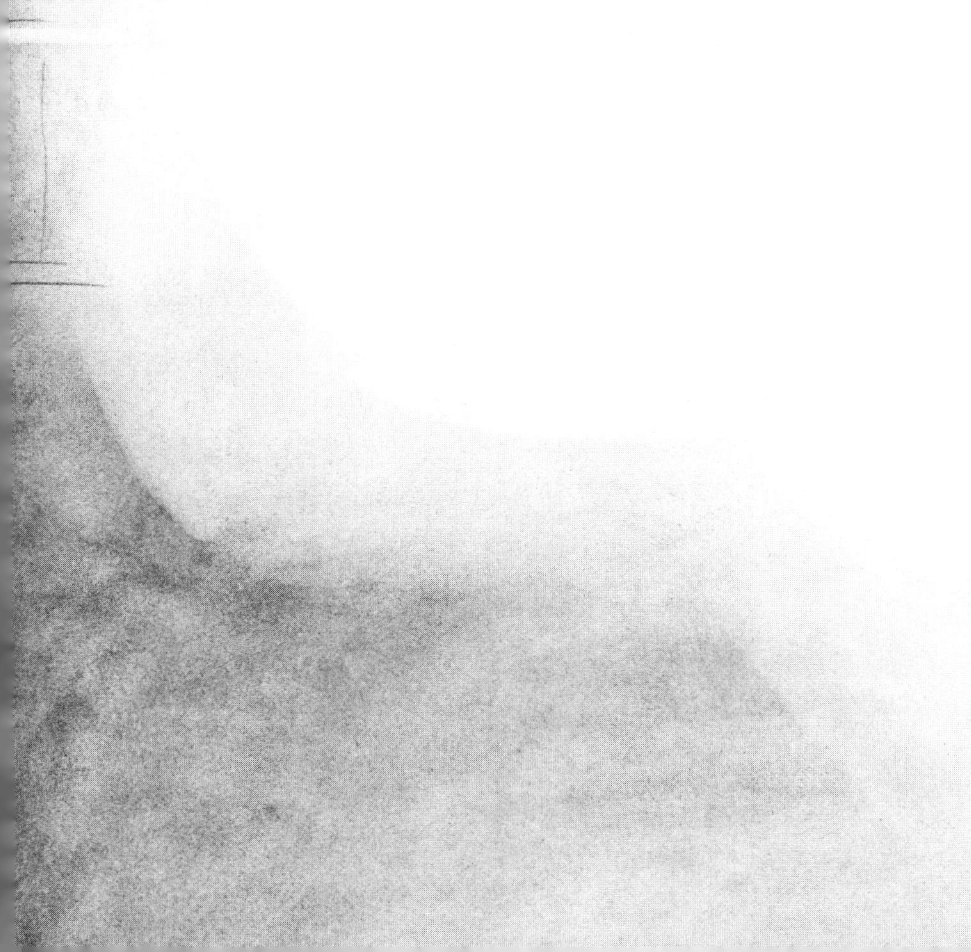

UNTIL I SAW THE SEA

Until I saw the sea
I did not know
that wind
could wrinkle water so.

I never knew
that sun
could splinter a whole sea of blue.

Nor
did I know before,
a sea breathes in and out
upon a shore.

—Lilian Moore

ROCKS

Big rocks into pebbles
Pebbles into sand.
I really hold a million million rocks here in my hand.

—Florence Parry Heide

PRETENDING TO SLEEP

Pretending to sleep
in the back seat
I squeeze my eyelids
like the wings
of a caught moth.
They flutter—
but I breathe deep.

I suck my cheeks in
so I can't grin
when they whisper,
"We won't wake her."
I'm a good faker.

—*Judith Thurman*

GONE

I've looked behind the shed
And under every bed:
I think he must be dead.

What reason for alarm?
He doesn't know the farm.
I *knew* he'd come to harm!

He was a city one
Who never had begun
To think the city fun.

Now where could he have got?
He doesn't know a lot.
I haven't heard a shot.

That old abandoned well,
I thought. Perhaps he fell?
He didn't. I could tell.

Perhaps he found a scent:
A rabbit. Off he went.
He'll come back home all spent.

Groundhogs, they say, can fight;
And raccoons will at night.
He'd not know one by sight!

I've called and called his name.
I'll never be the same.
I blame myself... I blame...

All *he* knows is the park;
And now it's growing dark.
A bark? *You hear a bark?*

—*David McCord*

THE STAR IN THE PAIL

I took the pail for water when the sun was high
And left it in the shadow of the barn nearby.

When evening slippered over like the moth's brown wing,
I went to fetch the water from the cool wellspring.

The night was clear and warm and wide, and I alone
Was walking by the light of stars as thickly sown

As wheat across the prairie, or the first fall flakes,
Or spray upon the lawn—the kind the sprinkler makes.

But every star was far away as far can be,
With all the starry silence sliding over me.

And every time I stopped I set the pail down slow,
For when I stooped to pick the handle up to go

Of all the stars in heaven there was one to spare,
And he silvered in the water and I left him there.

—*David McCord*

SO WILL I

My grandfather remembers long ago
the white Queen Anne's lace that grew wild.
He remembers the buttercups and goldenrod
from when he was a child.

He remembers long ago
the white snow falling falling.
He remembers the bluebird and thrush
at twilight
calling, calling.

He remembers long ago
the new moon in the summer sky
He remembers the wind in the trees
and its long, rising sigh.
And so will I
          so will I.

—*Charlotte Zolotow*

TOMORROW

It lives there
In one small corner of my head,
    Sailing sky to moon's ocean,
    Swimming green to ocean's deep,
    Dreaming new hours, new times.
    It bubbles, bursts a new explosion:

It is the growing up,
The tomorrow
Of me.

—Myra Cohn Livingston

IN THE PITCH OF THE NIGHT

In the pitch of the night,
where there isn't a light,
comes a very bad rabbit
with a horrible habit
of filling my head
with dangers—

    wanting to take me
    through forests
    where strangers
    and ghoulies
    high in the trees
    try to leap out at me.

So I say,
"Listen here, rabbit.
I'm sick of your habit.
I've had enough
of your nightmarish fright.

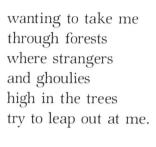

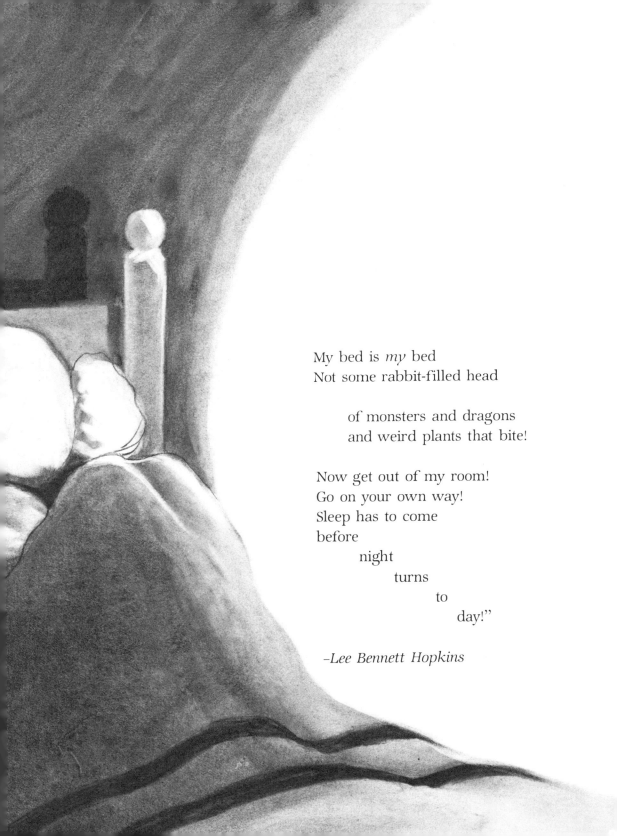

My bed is *my* bed
Not some rabbit-filled head

of monsters and dragons
and weird plants that bite!

Now get out of my room!
Go on your own way!
Sleep has to come
before
      night
           turns
                to
                    day!"

–Lee Bennett Hopkins

WHEN I AM ME

I'm impossible... possible,
breaking away from the
hard-holding hand
and flinging myself
in the air
on the sea
on a wave in the land.
And thrashing about
just impossibly... possibly,
calling—no, yelling—
as loud as I can,
I am me!
I am me!
I can do anything.
I can run
to the end of the land
if I want to
or swim to the end of the sea
if I want to.
      I want to—not now,
      but I want to
      and will when it's possible...
      really is possible.
      Everything's possible
      when I am me.

—*Felice Holman*

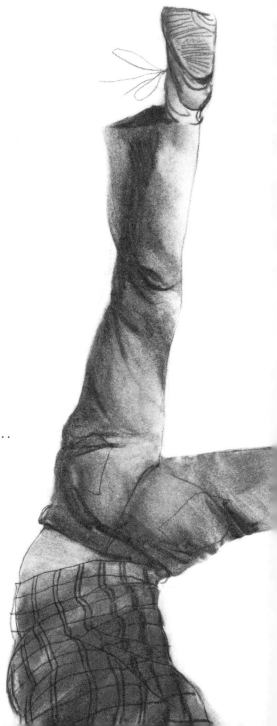

Lee Bennett Hopkins is well established in the world of children's literature. He has written novels for young people and edited several poetry collections, among them the A.L.A. Notable Book *Don't You Turn Back: Poems by Langston Hughes* and *Morning, Noon and Nighttime, Too.* His articles have been published in *Horn Book, Language Arts, English Journal,* and *Instructor,* and his column, "Book Bonanza," has appeared in *Teacher* magazine since 1974. In 1978 he chaired the Poetry Award Committee for the National Council of Teachers of English and currently serves as host/consultant for the award-winning television program *Zebra Wings.* He lives in Scarborough, New York.

Glo Coalson is a painter and sculptor who has illustrated over fifteen books for children in her warm, expressive style. She was born in Abilene, Texas, and has lived in New York and Kotzebue, Alaska, an Eskimo village north of the Arctic Circle. She now lives in Dallas.